From Pain to POWER

by
Dallas N. Gordon

From Pain to Power

First Printed in United Kingdom 2018

Published by Conscious Dreams Publishing

www.consciousdreamspublishing.com

ISBN: 978-1-912551-32-3

Dedicated to:

Dad. I'm forever grateful for your love.

Pain is temporary;
victory is forever.

Acknowledgements

I want to first thank my Creator who makes all things come together in my life for good. He orchestrates all things in the most perfect synchronicity.

Thank you, hubby, for putting up with me, accepting me completely and for being my biggest supporter and best friend. I love you forever.

Thank you, Dad, for being that constant force in my life. Thanks for loving me, protecting me and providing me with the chance to go further than you ever did. I get it now. I love and miss you every day.

Thank you, Mom, for your steadfast love and for never, ever giving up on me. Thanks for being the meaning of unfaltering, unconditional love. You are a true gem and I realize how blessed I am to call you Mom.

Thank you, bro. I'm grateful for you and your beautiful family. Thank you for covering me, setting a fine example and for being the best big brother I could ever ask for. You have no idea how much I admire you.

Thank you Shaun, Priya and Micah. All three of you are God's way of saying how much he loves and favors me. Everything I do is for you. You all inspire me daily to be my best self and Mommy loves you to the moon.

Thank you to my big Sis. God gives you just what you need in the exact moments that you need it. I truly appreciate you in my life.

I appreciate my extended family: my mom-in-law and sisters who accept me as their own. I'm grateful to two friends in particular, who gave me that nudge to write my first book. I want to thank Valencia Daniels and Renée Purdie for helping me push the limits and complete this project. You ladies rock and I love you to the moon.

A big 'ole thank you to my mentor, Jermaine Steele, for seeing greatness in me when I didn't have the full scope of it myself.

And I want to give a special thanks to my very close friends whom I hold dear. You all are phenomenal women and literally motivate me every single day. I love you all very deeply. Thank you for believing in me.

Hopefully, I haven't left anyone out, but there are so many people who continue to impact my journey and were catalysts in helping me arrive to this very moment. Thank you.

My final thanks to Conscious Dreams Publishing. Thank you for believing in my story and helping me bring it to life.

Contents

Introduction

**In every negative, a positive exists.
The question is, will you find it?**

Ever found yourself in a place where the pain in your life was unbearable? Do you know brokenness, heartache and disappointment all too well? Do you throw your hands up in the air at times and say: "This is it! Can't life just give me a break?" Are you feeling like a dark cloud hovers everywhere you go and it seems you've been waiting forever and a day for the sun to shine again?

I, too, have found myself at my lowest point during these trying times. Life didn't seem to be taking my side. I would give and give, sacrifice and give some more. I lived my life uprightly. I was deemed to be a pretty good person. Even after doing these things, I still felt life had been unjust to me.

What do you do when you've given all you have and your well begins to run dry? What do you do when you constantly show up for others, but when you need them, they're nowhere to be found? What do you do when you open your mouth, but can't utter another prayer? Where do you turn when life seems to be breaking all around you and it becomes fragments, pieces of an all too confusing puzzle?

Life changes, and when it does, it tends to change us. As time progresses, we may be hard pressed. We have the choice to go and grow with life or the choice to become resistant to change. I have found it's through our pain that we experience a change in perspective, and through it we evolve and become better people.

Getting better – not bitter – is what this book is all about.

In life, there will be many highs and lows. The lows aren't fun, but if it weren't for those seasons we wouldn't be the people we are today. During our seasons of pain, we find that the most growth happens. If we learn to embrace our valleys, we can grow leaps and bounds, learn meaningful life lessons and heal the world around us. This book is about learning to survive hard times, being grateful when the going gets tough and finding purpose in painful seasons.

To be transparent, I have had some real low points in life. Situations die, people pass away and life has major let downs and changes. I've lost material things, lost someone dear to me and have had to pick up and rebuild what I considered to be my life multiple times. Each event was a major turning point and breakthrough in my life. Each time was just what I needed. Each time I came out better, refined.

Over time, I've learned that some situations aren't meant to be resurrected. Sometimes we are meant to reset and start again. I want people to know that there is life after death. And when I say death, I'm not just referencing the loss of a loved one, but am also speaking of major turning points and roadblocks.

In life, pain is inevitable; suffering, however, is optional. We'll experience painful seasons, but with the right change in perspective we can survive them, come out stronger and impact others while growing. This book is meant to help you cope and find purpose during painful seasons. I've learned that major setbacks lead to strong comebacks!

Chapter 1:
When it Rains, it Pours

I'll never forget the phone call I received on the day that changed everything. My mom was on the other end screaming; crying. The sound of helplessness in her voice. The man she loved for over 40 years had changed in an instant and was staring at her emotionless; blank. As she cried through the phone, my mind raced, reaching for the words to comfort her. The years with my dad flashed before me and I knew deep within after that moment, things would never be the same.

I've often wondered, during seasons of pain, why one misfortune doesn't seem to be enough in and of itself. Why do our misfortunes need to be accompanied by one heartbreak after the other? One disappointment after the last? For sure, I could handle one problem at a time. I could reach for the strength to handle just one, but problems always seemed to arrive in droves. I've lain awake many nights asking God, "Why?" I've wondered how in a matter of seconds, life as we know it can change in an instant and we end up faced with a completely new set of circumstances. I've always admired my mom. So strong, seemingly able to handle everything that came her way. During this season, I witnessed her literally just about break.

Let's go back in time

When my dad got sick it, it happened so suddenly and there was no time to brace ourselves or emotionally prepare. Just the summer before, we were all in Florida, my dad, mom, husband, our kids and I. All of us there laughing and having fun in the sun. Doing what we always did. I never could have imagined in just a short year later, Dad would be gone so quickly. Life and death are supernatural experiences that can leave us speechless, joyful, in awe, lost, broken-hearted or even confused. Life and death have no regard or respect for anyone. They can happen to anyone at any point in time. They just happen.

Unfortunately, it isn't until someone leaves and life as we know it is altered, that we realize just how much of a force they were in our lives. My dad, was that constant voice of reason. I look back over the pictures; the memories. Every party, every celebration, my dad was always there pictured with us. He wasn't the loudest in the room. He wasn't the life of the party. But he was that constant support. Always present. Always there. He was the rock of the family. We had gotten so used to leaning on him that we didn't realize at the time just how blessed we were to have him around.

Dad and me at my wedding

I was the female version of Dad. We had the same dimples. We shared the same laughs. I remember, Dad and I would get into these long drawn out conversations about music. We would converse about our favorite artists and break out in song. We would get lost in our own little world. We had our jokes that only he and I could understand. We had our ups and downs. Our loving moments and our not so loving moments. But at the end of every single day, one thing was for sure: we loved each other unconditionally. Who would I share those father-daughter moments with, now? There was no feeling I'd ever had in this whole wide world that compared to the devastation I felt. My heart was crushed, and I felt it physically.

Watching a loved one suffer and wither away is one of the most helpless feelings ever and a feeling I'd never wish on anyone. I'd visit my dad, whom I was just laughing with some days ago, and see him sitting there lifeless, without hope. This wasn't the man who raised me. It wasn't the man who taught me just about everything I know about faith. He dropped his fists and hung up his boxing gloves. He was simply tired of fighting. Each day I visited, I was searching for hope in his eyes. I was searching for signs of his will to live but I didn't find it. It took courage to place my own feelings and desires aside to fully understand and embrace what my dad wanted. That was to cross over and leave this life behind. I had to take all the love within and support his decision. I wanted for him to experience the best possible transition with my full support and understanding.

It was shortly after my dad passed that I felt I'd lost my faith. I believed God turned his back on Dad or, maybe even worse, covered His eyes. What would I do? I was Daddy's little girl. Who would fill his shoes? Losing him made me feel abandoned, like a child left in the middle of the road holding her teddy bear.

And it doesn't stop there... I know you're probably wondering, "Wow, what else?" I promise, this gets better. Hang in here with me. Remember, I mentioned how tragedies seem to partner up and don't arrive alone? On top of the strain that losing my dad had put on our family, old issues resurfaced. Like my life wasn't falling apart enough. I had reached the boiling point. You know, that point when the fire gets so hot that you can't stand it. I can't say that I completely broke, but my faith definitely needed repair. I was just tired. I guess I had struggled for so long, I think I felt I was getting negatives in return for all my positives and I didn't deserve it. I felt disappointment. I felt anger. I asked God frequently, "Why is all this happening to me? I don't deserve this!"

My husband (my blessing) and I have always helped other people — financially especially. We have opened up our home to family members in need and took the attitude that if we had it, everybody we loved had it too. To make a long sad story short, a past relationship ended with a string of ugly custody battles. My husband and I had spent entirely too much time, energy and money in court because of this seemingly never-ending disagreement. That's huge financial distress: $1,000 here, $2,500 there, and the bills constantly adding up. When it rains, it pours. The troubles kept piling on in heaps. Things breaking around the house: That's money. Automobiles needing repair: That's money. Garnishments for debts owed: That's money. It seemed everyone under the sun that could come for us, CAME.

On the emotional side, I'd done all I could to be the best mother to my son, never talking negatively about his dad. I'd done good even when it hurt. I'd gone over and beyond even when the other party wasn't providing or helping. I did good things, even when no one was watching. I would tell my son positive things, despite the negative things that were being said about me. I "reached for higher" even when I was being torn down and talked about. And yet, 14 years later, I was still being dragged through the mud and I wondered, "When will it ever end?" I was hoping that one day I would wake up from this nightmare of a dream and all the smoke would have cleared. I went months without uttering a word in prayer or to anyone else for that matter. I was too afraid that once I spoke, the words that escaped my mouth would be full of such anger, such negativity that those words would be the end of me. They would end any chance I had to get over this; get through this. What's left to do when you've done all you can and life still isn't aligning the way you envisioned? What do you do when your prayers seem to go unanswered?

Chapter 2:
Daybreak

When I lifted my pen to start writing this book, my turning point began. It was as I wrote these words that I decided my suffering was going to count for something. After many cloudy days and extended periods of darkness, I was rescued by a quick glimpse of the sun. That small glimpse of sun was all I needed to remind me that God hadn't left and hope was still alive.

The unexpected will always happen in life; there will always be conditions beyond our control and those things we don't understand. Deep within the darkness of our uncertainties there's a force deep down inside, that gentle whisper of a voice reminding us that we've got strength left, even if it's just a little.

Tap into a strength that's greater than your own.

A minister friend said it best. She spoke these words and I hung onto every one. She said, "When you lose all hope, you only need faith the size of a mustard seed. When you can't pray, when you're weathering the storm and have no belief left, all you need is a little tiny bit of faith. Reach for that small bit and trust God. When you do this, boy, does your situation move."

When I was at my breaking point, the only thing sustaining me was that supernatural strength and small bit of faith she spoke about. Even though I was going through a rough time, I still treated my family with love. I still ran my businesses every day. I still put a smile on my face and broadcasted before hundreds of people, encouraging them to never give up. How was I able to continue to do all this when my own life felt like a disaster? I reached out beyond myself and tapped into my super power, that strength that was greater than my own.

Hands off!

Oftentimes, when trouble comes, we rely on ourselves, our own minds and our own ability to do the fixing. We figure if we could just have a bit more blessings and a little less pain, life would be much better. Trying one by one, we scratch our heads trying to put the pieces of the puzzle together until we realize that they don't quite fit and our backs are against the wall. When I find myself in these dark moments and I'm at a loss for what to do, I find it best to do nothing at all. When my hands are all over situations, I tend to make more of a mess. When I realize that maybe I don't have the tools to do all the fixing and take my hands OFF, the pieces come flying together with ease. When you're backed in a corner and feeling helpless, hands off! Take your hands off the problem, trust that the Creator will provide and it will work out just fine. When's the last time you released and took those hands off?

I remember being mentally exhausted, tired and worn down from trying to figure out the perfect course of action. It wasn't until I let go and realized that this situation was out of my control that I began to see a little light at the end of the tunnel.

"All things work together for the good of those that love Him, and are called according to His purpose." — Romans 8:28

Rest assured, that everything will work out for your good. When you're going through tough times, it's often hard to see your way out. When trouble comes, we hit the panic button. We panic because we can't get in full view of the sun. When we see that glimpse of sun, we look back and realize that it was going to be just fine all along. There is a much greater plan at work, and in trying times we can rest in knowing nothing lasts forever and the best is yet to come.

The solution was already set in stone. Your victory was won before the problem began. Even if you can only see that very small glimpse of the sun and your faith is smaller than mustard seed, rest and know that it's already done; it's already settled.

Why worry?

When I'm unsure of the outcome and uncertainties plague me, I tend to worry. In the middle of the night, on those nights I can't sleep, is when I worry most. I sit in the dark with my thoughts and play out the scenarios, trying to figure ways out of my discomfort.

Worry is a negative emotion. It starts bad and ends bad. Worry festers and grows when we're uncomfortable in the moment and anxious about what tomorrow holds.

Many years ago, anxiety got the best of me. I was so wound up from the day to day chaos that I couldn't handle even the slightest turbulence. I bounced from doctor to doctor seeking a solution to the nervous energy that I harbored within day after day. Now that time has passed and I'm standing on the other side, I look back and realize that it was worry that led me there. Worry will lead you to emotional and physical instability, and living for tomorrow is one of the major causes of worry. I'm grateful that eventually I began working my way out of the state I was in and I'm convinced that you can too.

Does worry plague you? Here's some food for thought.

Between 98% and 99.9% of the things we worry about will never ever happen. When we allow worry to have its way with us; crying, losing sleep and missing opportunities to enjoy life, 98% of what's robbing us from our happiness will never occur.

Just recently, I was worried sick about something, so I asked a few friends for prayer. Soon after, I found out that the entire time I was worrying, the situation had already diffused itself. When we worry, we compromise our peace and give a lot of something for absolutely nothing in return.

Will worrying change the outcomes? No, never.

Let's challenge our challenges and ask this question when we're tempted to worry: "Will my worrying change this?"

The answer we find will always be the same: Worrying won't change situations and stress will only destroy your peace.

> *"Once you accept, truly accept, that stuff will happen to you and there is nothing you can do about it, stress miraculously leaves your life"* — Srikumar Rao

A dear friend of mind said something very profound one day as we were chatting over the phone. She said, "Do not give energy to the outcomes that you do not want." What she was saying was that when we put energy into worrying about outcomes, we welcome those outcomes to manifest into our reality.

Focus your energy on what you DO want to happen.

We aren't in control of what tomorrow holds, so why even try to be? As a matter of fact, tomorrow may never come. One of the greatest lessons I've learned is that life is not promised. Why worry when we could spend more time enjoying the moment and infusing the atmosphere with positive thoughts?

Now is the only moment that we have.

There's power when we relinquish control and cast all of our worries into the hands of the Creator. We may not always have the know-how to undo what's been done. We may not always feel we have the strength to carry on. But it's in those moments, when we're being swallowed in the darkness, that we look up and see that small glimpse of sun.

Chapter 3:
Permission

Rewind

When my dad passed, I was devastated. I wasn't sure how exactly to respond, so for a while, I had no response. I just went about, taking life as it came, in silence. Not speaking much about his passing or how it made me feel. I also felt that I needed to stay strong, at least for my mom. I wanted to be a support for her during her time of loss, so I held my emotions inside.

Since I hadn't shed a tear, I thought I was over it. But I still felt a great deal of pain and sorrow. I was too afraid to face myself; too afraid to grieve. I didn't give myself permission to express how the loss made me feel. It wasn't until I began speaking out, that I started to feel some sense of relief. I began processing my pain by speaking out to help others.

In a strange way, the process of my grieving motivated me, but that's because I allowed it to. I thought about all that that my father wanted me to be, like more outspoken. It was during that time that I broke out of my shell. I went almost overnight from shy introvert to speaking my truth with boldness. I realized, that life as we know it, is not promised. The time to take action is now! I put procrastination to bed and I've been in motion ever since.

The amazing thing was, by operating outside of my comfort zone, many were impacted in a positive way. The people around me had no clue that I had been grieving all along in silence. I had no idea of the ripple effect that my speaking out would cause. Speaking out, despite my pain and shifting the focus towards those in need, in turn helped me through my own grieving process.

For those grieving a loss, be it a marriage, career or loved one,
I'd like to share my grieving process with you.
I believe that in my sharing, you too will give yourself
permission to feel and work your own way
through to a path of healing.

Acknowledge that it's real:

The first step is to acknowledge that it is real. Speaking from my own experience, my father's passing was so unreal to me. I did not want to accept that my dad was gone. It was sudden, unfair, and frankly I was mad at God about it. It's a bad thing to say, I know, but I was. It's important to acknowledge the fact that it's happened, there's nothing you can do to change it and accept **all** the feelings that come along with it.

Give yourself permission:

It's important to give yourself permission to feel and allow yourself to shamelessly grieve. I shared a little earlier, that I didn't feel it was okay to speak about my grief or to let the tears and emotions flow. I felt I had to be strong for others, so in turn, I denied myself the time and space to grieve. It doesn't matter if you feel angry, confused, or if you want to question God. It is what it is in that moment. Let yourself just BE in the current moment. Allow the tears; the emotions; the grief to just happen. Allow yourself the right to grieve.

Do it your own way:

Next, allow yourself to grieve *in your own way*. I've witnessed each of my family members express their grief differently. At first, I don't think my mom gave herself permission to cry. Many times, we convince ourselves we have to be strong and don't allow ourselves permission to feel sorrow. You can't keep grief at bay forever. Not giving full expression to how you're feeling can be destructive in the future.

Talk about it when it's time:

There will come a time when you'll need to talk about it. Initially, I wouldn't discuss it. For a minute, well, a lot of minutes, I was grieving silently. My friends were calling me. My family members were calling me. Everyone was trying to comfort me (or find comfort themselves) and I refused to receive calls or consolation from anyone. I couldn't bring myself to speak about what happened. I was hurt so deeply; I could barely speak. Many people shut themselves off from the world after experiencing a loss and I did just that.

With that said, when the debilitating part of grief starts to ease, and you start feeling "stuck," this is a good time for you to open up and talk with someone you can trust. If there is no one trustworthy in your circle, maybe a pastor or professional can be a listening ear. Refusing to open up and keeping feelings trapped within can cause greater problems down the road.

Welcome change and embrace the new:

The new has come and old things have passed away. Don't be afraid to forge new paths and push your limits. Meet new people, visit new places and do things you've never done before. Be open to trying anything POSITIVE. A new environment, new people, new scenery. Think new!

> "*There is a sacredness in tears. They are not the mark of weakness, but of power. They speak more eloquently than ten thousand tongues. They are the messengers of overwhelming grief, of deep contrition, and of unspeakable love.*" — Washington Irving

Chapter 4:
Choices

Life is choice-driven. It's hard to admit, but being in unrelenting emotional pain is essentially a choice. In every situation, there are negatives and positives. In every heartbreak, there is a lesson. The question is, are you willing to learn?

Unfortunately, everyone will experience pain at some point. Some will make the choice to learn the lesson and others won't make this choice.

I found my peace when I began focusing on the lesson and being grateful within the process. What I'm going to say next may tempt you to toss this book aside, but stay with me. When you make the choice to turn the negative experiences into learning experiences, that's when your suffering will ease.

Our greatest weapon against unease, is our ability to choose one thought over another.

When trouble showed up, I could have chosen to throw in the towel, drop my head and give up. Instead, I chose to to do the opposite and began speaking my truth. I wanted others to realize, that sometimes life throws curve balls that can't be avoided. When shots are fired, they hurt, BAD. It was never promised that all of our sorrows would disappear in the single passing of a night.

We may not be able to change what happens to us but we can change our response to what happens.

Could we lower our heads, and allow our crowns to slip? Yes, indeed, we could! Could we remain in silence and allow pity to have its way? Yes, we certainly could! However, if we give in to the pressures of this world, we'd only continue sinking until we drown. Instead, we have the alternative to make the shift, take up our crowns and do just the opposite. We can make the choice to begin allowing our pain to fuel our power. We can choose to allow those things which we can't control to teach us and propel us towards greatness.

But what if I choose to stay stuck?

Choosing to stay stuck can be compared to tying a large rope around your neck with a huge rock attached and jumping overboard. When we make the choice to remain "stuck", we're writing ourselves a death wish. We're spinning our wheels but going nowhere.

I recently listened to an interview of a runner without legs. He was asked during the interview how he encourages himself when he feels like giving up. His response: he reminds himself that it's disrespectful to give up. If he gave up, all his momma's sacrifices would be in vain. If he gave up, all the children who look up to him, that are depending on his success so that they too can have the faith to succeed, would lose hope. When you choose to stay stuck, you choose to sabotage the purpose and plan for your life. When you choose not to move forward, you also affect all those around you who you would be paving the way for. When you allow the winds of this life to blow you off course, not only have you robbed yourself of experiencing and living out your true purpose in life, but you're also hindering your purpose and causing others around you to also be hindered.

This journey you're on, even the good, the bad and the ugly, it's not in vain. Your suffering and the power within you to overcome is bigger than you. The choice you make to shift and grow affects the world around you. I've had to realize, that my victory is not just my own. This victory also belongs to all those who have been strategically placed on my path. If I give up, what happens to them? Do you see just how powerful this is?

I know what you may be thinking, and I agree, "it's easier said than done". Anyone can tell you, "I know it was terrible, that thing that happened to you in the past. But it's a new day. Just get over it." But unless they've lived in your shoes; felt what you felt, it's always going to be easier said than done.

In case you're feeling stuck, and can't just seem to get pass that massive let down in your past. If no one ever told you, I'm here to tell you that you ARE somebody. Not just any ole body, but someone great. There's a reason you were created and there's a divine reason you're here on this earth. All that you've been through up until now, is an intricate part of your purpose in life. I'd say, you ought not allow any problem or person stand in your way of becoming all you can be.

Your challenges are only as great as the giant you'll become.

As I lay awake one night, I found myself asking God ...

"Why? Why is all this falling down around me so fast? All I see is brokenness. I've given of my time, my talents; my money. I'm not perfect, but I've done my best to live uprightly and be faithful. Why me, Lord? Why me?"

The answer: Your challenges are only as great as your fullest potential. There is no need for someone who isn't great to be faced with great giants. Great people are faced with the greatest of obstacles because they require more fine tuning, more refining; more strength to walk fully in the purpose they've been perfectly made for.

" *I stopped asking, "Why me?", and I started to say, "Try me"* — unknown

We can't choose our giants in life and our giants (problems) appear to choose us. But we can choose how we respond to the trouble in our lives. We all have a purpose, tailor-made just for us and giants arrive to bump us off the great path. It's time we looked those giants directly in the eye and remind them of just how strong we really are.

As long as we exercise the power of choice, these little "G's" (giants) can't overtake us. We can choose to win on the battlefield of our minds OR we can choose to allow these problems to defeat us. I'll let you in on a little secret: *Once we trade our pain for the lesson, and realize we're being sharpened for a greater purpose, we can't be defeated.*

Remember, despite all you've been through, life is choice driven. So why not choose life? We have a choice to reach out beyond our pain and when we do, others gain awareness and are impacted. Although pain is unavoidable, through that pain a deep lesson can be learned if you allow for reflection and understanding. If you change your perspective and ask, "Okay, God, what can I learn from this? How can I grow from this? Who can I help?" That's when you begin to reach outside of yourself. That's when your breakthrough is on the horizon. In the midst of your PAIN, others get positively impacted. In the midst of your PAIN, that's when you get clarity.

" *To make it right, **pain** and suffering is the key to all windows, without it, there is no way of life."* — Angelina Jolie

" *Your **pain** is the breaking of the shell that encloses your understanding."* — Khalil Gibran

" ***Pain** is temporary. It may last a minute, or an hour, or a day, or a year, but eventually it will subside and something else will take its place. If I quit, however, it lasts forever."* — Lance Armstrong

Chapter 5:
Turning Point

Change happens when we begin to ask ourselves the right questions. I began noticing continual transformations within myself once I started asking questions like:

How can I improve from this?
How can I change my perception of this?
What positives can come of this?
How can I GROW from this?

A Flash in the Past

The first real setback in my adult life was a failed past relationship. I was pretty young when we got together despite the fact that everyone around me advised against it. Honestly, looking back on it now, I have no idea what made me do it. I guess I made decisions prematurely due to my immaturity at the time. I was raised in a strict Christian home and didn't have much room to color outside of the lines growing up. I ran off with the first guy I could date as soon as I finished high school and prematurely said, "I DO". I had no idea the effects this decision would have on my life and the repercussions I'd experience years after. To make a long story short, there were many ups and downs; we found ourselves in divorce court in what seemed like overnight, and I ended up pregnant at a young age with my now eldest son. I did my best, even going back to "try again" after divorcing and gave it my best shot. In the end, I was emotionally and mentally drained from trying.

That period of my life was a real rough patch. Trying to overcompensate in a relationship that was lacking emotional health and stability really took its toll on me. My extended stay was due to my having a child with this man. In my mind, it was the right thing to do. I'd grown up in a two parent home and expected nothing less for my son. I never imagined I'd be a 20-year-old single mom.

The aftereffect of that season in my life was extreme anxiety. I wasn't capable of processing daily life. I didn't like being alone. I didn't like going outside. Let's just say, I didn't come out of that relationship the way I went in. I wasn't that girl my parents worked so hard to raise. I lost weight, I lost my hair; I was losing me. I was unraveling fast and extremely afraid of what my tomorrow would bring.

My parents were my rock during that time. My son and I left, the relationship was over and I needed recovering. Thank God for parents who continue to parent even after their children are grown. Thank the good Lord for a praying momma. I literally had to rebuild my life. I lost everything, well, everything I thought I had at that time. I also felt I'd brought great shame upon my Christian family.

I really had to go back to the drawing board and begin my period of re-self-discovery. I had to start fresh and learn who it was God meant for me to be. I knew that something was missing and that something had driven me to the place I then was. I soon discovered what that missing something was: self-love. I loved my family, my friends, my child, but did I love me? This thought had never crossed my mind up until that moment.

Even then, my turning point began when I stopped to ask myself questions that mattered. I asked myself questions like: "How did I get in this situation? Why did I allow this person into my life?" My thoughts sent me on a seeking rampage and I ended up borrowing a library book on self-love. It was during a bus trip to Atlantic City, as I flipped the pages of that book, when it all hit home for me. When you don't love yourself, you allow less than loving people and situations into your life. The outcomes you attract are only reflections of your personal perception. I sat there on that bus in complete awe; in silence. I knew, after that trip to Atlantic City, my life would never be the same.

I had to pick up the pieces of my entire life — and then figure out how to put them back together again. After all, I had another person's life depending on me. Through this process, I discovered that it's not selfish to love yourself. For the rest of our lives, we'll continually be learning about ourselves and we'll forever be seeking better ways to love ourselves. When it came down to self-love, I had to start from ground zero, and work my way to the top (and I'm still working, by the way). But it all started with asking the right questions.

Questions are catalysts for change. Never stop asking.

How do I care for myself?
How do I love myself?
How do I build myself up to the point
that I never allow this to happen to me again?

I went to great lengths during that time to consciously build myself up. First, I had to halt my negative patterns, and one of them was the expectation of meeting the perfect someone who'd "fix" my brokenness. One of the worst things a person can do is apply temporary Band-Aids. When we don't make an effort to fix issues within ourselves, we only go out there and attract the same problems — and sometimes they are even worse. When you don't pause, reflect and choose to learn the lesson, you make it impossible for yourself to end negative patterns.

Unfortunately, I went through a series of attracting negative, bad relationships into my reality. Each guy I dated may have had one-single quality better than the last, but overall, the attempted relationships were broken from the start. The broken relationships cycle only reminded me of the fact that I was broken myself. I just didn't realize it was me that needed fixing.

The stretch of dating and skating through different relationships led me right back where I began. I thought someone new would end the agony I felt, but this thinking only landed me right back into the arms of my ex. Yes, I actually went back to someone I'd previously divorced and started a life with him (again). We lived together for about three years. Three long years! And honestly, the day I set foot in that house, I knew I'd made the wrong choice. But I stayed for three long years struggling to fix something that had been broken beyond repair. Which brings me to this point:

Some situations are never meant to be resurrected. They are meant to be left dead — buried.

One morning, after I woke, I made a final decision to leave for good. This time, however, I was stronger. I was no longer that insecure girl I was three years earlier. And I've never looked back since.

Once I exited that phase of my life, I put a pause on entering new relationships and shifted the focus to the one I was developing with myself. It was just like the first stages in a new relationship with a new person, instead I had lots to learn about myself.

I kept on asking...

What do I want?
What do I like?
What makes me happy?
What makes me smile?

I didn't know how to answer any of these questions. Yet.

When I was going through my worst period, I was a nervous wreck and nothing helped. I went to counseling, took medication and cried out to God more times than I could count. I give thanks every day for my mom. She refused to give up on me. She would give me Scripture on top of Scripture, and she was praying with me every day. If you took a glance at my right hand, it would shake — and it wasn't from my morning coffee.

I'd talk to God and say, *"I don't know what to do. I don't know what's going to help me."* Even though I was young, I felt I didn't have a chance at life. I never thought I'd marry again, especially after the state the last marriage left me in.

Slowly but surely, I stopped worrying about tomorrow and started living in the now moment. I found enjoyment in getting out on my own and began looking at life from a new perspective. I'd developed a new appreciation and connection with nature. I would go out for jogs (and I still do), long nature walks and appreciate the little things. I'd look up at the sky and the world around me with a new found appreciation for all things. The trees, the birds, my eyes, my legs, my feet, my hands, my smile; I expressed gratitude for each of them. I began looking myself in the mirror and telling myself just how beautiful I was every single day.

These small daily changes sparked my turning point. I started out as the girl anxiously anticipating her future and transformed into a confident, calm and secure woman. A woman who was learning to love herself. I promised myself, from that moment on, that I wouldn't allow just anyone in my life, because the price was much too great. I began to guard my own heart.

I started speaking life into my own existence and affirming positively to myself. I began facing new challenges head on and asking myself in each situation, *"If I do this, am I demonstrating self-love?"* My answer to this question was a catalyst for change: *"If me doing this isn't loving myself, then I don't need it."*

I began establishing boundaries and making decisions for myself that were best for ME, my emotions and my well-being. I put my foot down, got comfortable with the word, *"NO"*, and became less concerned with other people's opinions. I was where I needed to be; doing what I needed to do. I was busy watering my own grass. I embraced inner healing and started falling in love with myself. During this time, I gained the strength to begin the rebuilding process. I'm grateful that from that point on, the cycle of attracting negative people and situations into my life had broken. I was free!

We can miss out on a deeper meaning if we choose to focus on the suffering rather than the lesson. I could have chosen to rehearse the memories from my negative past over and over, instead I chose to focus forward. I chose to rise above the pain. I made the choice to seek answers, grow and accept the lesson. I chose to redirect my energy and ask the right questions. I began to shift.

"Turn your wounds into wisdom." — Oprah Winfrey

Chapter 6:
God Has Not Forgotten

I want you to know that despite what you're going through you are not forgotten and you are not forsaken. Have you ever asked: *"God, what's going on? Have you forgotten me? I'm tired of the winds blowing and the boat rocking. I'm at my breaking point and I'm about ready to give up. Seems I'm always last in line and sitting on the sidelines watching everyone else get blessed. What about me? When's it going to be my time?"*

Although it seems God's favor has passed you by, in reality, you're not the last to the finish line.

Your time is right now! Right now is the right time for you to be blessed!

All those good deeds you've done, those times you could have spoken a negative word, in moments you gave your last, and you gave your best. Even when you walked the straight and narrow when no one was looking… God saw.

While pain is inevitable, suffering is indeed optional. Suffering or how you process discomfort is a reflection of your mindset. If you can change your mind, you can change your life.

Pain is inevitable. Suffering is optional.

Change your perspective and change your results.

You may be asking, "but how do I change my perspective when everything seems to be going wrong?" Change happens when we begin perceiving things differently and thinking different thoughts, one thought at a time.

Begin…

Expecting more.

Believing more.

Tell yourself, *"This is going to lead to better days."*

Hang on a little bit longer.

Lift your head up just a bit higher. Don't let it hang too low or you won't be able to see the opportunities ahead.

Think about your lowest point and ask yourself if you overcame it. Did you get over the hurdle? Did that dark season last forever? The Creator did it then and He'll do it again and again, and then, once more!

This time around, your blessing is going to be even greater. You're going to come out even stronger. Purified. On a higher level. The struggle was great but the blessings will be greater.

When you're feeling discouraged, alone and want to throw in the towel, think on these things:

1. When you feel like giving up, remember you haven't been forgotten or forsaken. When the fire gets hot, it's a sure sign that you're on the right track. If it were easy, everyone would be a success. Success is available for everyone but everyone won't achieve great success. It happens for the chosen few who DECIDE to remain still, keep their feet planted and who refuse to be moved.
2. Look back to your times of triumph. If you've been tested before and passed with flying colors, you'll do it again. You are not last and surely not forgotten. The blessings that are in store for you are for you only.

3. Have faith that there is a plan for you and it will come into fruition. Revelations come during troubled times. You learn more about yourself, what you're made of and who God is.
4. Pain is inevitable, but suffering is optional. Suffering is a state of mind. Whether one suffers or not is a choice. Remember, your comeback will be greater than your setback (if you choose). Look your problems in the eye and remain steadfast.
5. Make a firm decision that no matter what happens you're moving ahead. Remain persistent despite what it looks like. Focus forward and march yourself right into victory.
6. Stop worrying about the things you cannot control. When has worrying ever changed a thing? Worrying only leads to a heavy heart and restless nights. While we can't control every situation, we CAN control our response to pain, setbacks and disappointments.
7. Replace the thinking: *"things should be different from the way they are now"* with the affirmation: *"I am at the right place at the right time. The timing in my life is perfect."* Take life day by day and in the "now" moment. Embrace it. Focus on what you can create today.
8. Repair relationships. If you haven't talked to that family member in years and you know you need to patch things up, don't hesitate to pick up the phone or pay them a visit. Don't hold back the words: *"I love you"*. If you don't try, you'll never know. Do your part to repair broken relationships. Do your best by the people you love and make amends within your heart. Life is not promised.

"Can a woman forget her nursing child and not have compassion on the son of her womb? Surely they may forget, Yet I will not forget you. See, I have inscribed you on the palms of My hands; your walls are continually before Me. Your sons shall make haste; your destroyers and those who laid you waste shall go away from you." — Isaiah 49:12-17

Chapter 7:
Push

The right time is NOW!

There's no time like the present. Why?

Tomorrow is not promised. Life can change in the blinking of an eye and all we have is now.

We'll never know just how much time we have, so now's the time to PUSH. There are times when our foundation will be shaken. Every disappointment will seem to arrive at once, and all with one common agenda: to distract you from purpose and knock you off course.

Life may jerk and shove you around, but when this happens we must PUSH BACK! When I push through what I'm going through despite how I feel, something magical happens. Not only are others blessed because of my faithfulness but I, in turn, am blessed too. I feel a rush over me, a release; an overwhelming positive feeling that everything will be alright. When I push through my emotions and still rise to the occasion, I receive an extra push; I receive an extra dose of faith. It's similar to the video games that I watch my kids play. When the character is out of energy, they need a power ball; a supercharge; a lifeline; a push. This surge of power seems to show up in a very similar way; when I push through my pain to help others, I receive that extra "push" of power.

Say this with me. *"I only have now. I have only right now to fulfill my purpose. I have the power to push through to my breakthrough. I am living fully in the now moment."*

Make this moment a moment of NOW. Divorce your excuses and say *"I do"* to your purpose and passions. Say "NO" to allowing yourself to remain crippled by past hurts any longer.

Now's the time to push through the pain and answer the call in the NOW moment. There's someone out there that needs to hear your story; your life experiences. They need to know you survived it. They need an extra surge of strength. When they hear your testimony, it will give them the power to push through the pain and show up in their own lives stronger than ever before.

Sometimes the journey we must travel seems much further than we can bare. Every single second of a drought season feels agonizing. You may need to crawl again, kick, cry, even scream. Do whatever you need as long as you don't quit!

When you take the high road, despite the negatives, and push through anyway, the blessings show up.

Remember, you're in complete control of what you say, do and how you take action. You are in the driver's seat of your own life. If you don't drive, you're allowing life to just happen to you instead of YOU happening to it. Don't be the person that sits and waits around for the change to come. You BE the change. Show up, push through and make change happen.

Oftentimes, we need a reminder of what or whom we're showing up for. When I don't feel like going forward I ask myself, *"What's my why?"* I remind myself that if I don't show up I could risk letting my family down. My kids and husband believe in me and expect me to keep climbing. If I don't keep it moving, I could be giving up on my purpose in life and that could adversely affect all the lives that will change as a result of fulfilling that purpose. If I don't push through, I could risk having to live with the pain of regret and disappointment that I let myself and family down, when all I had to do was make a single choice. If we don't show up and follow our own path in our own shoes, think about it: who will show up for us? Who's going to do us better than we can?

In times when you feel like you don't have the strength to PUSH, remember:

- Nobody can do YOU the way that YOU can
- Life can change in the blinking of an eye. All we have is the NOW moment
- There's someone out there that will experience their breakthrough all because you pushed through
- You have the power within to overcome

"*Life does not happen to you; it happens for you!*" — Jim Carrey

Life is waiting for you to show up and be the star. Life happens when you push, show up strong and make it happen.

Trouble happens and when it does, instead of tarrying there, turn your pain into a positive. The best time to show up for yourself is within the NOW moment. Don't give up. Push!

Chapter 8:
The Antidote

Start Counting

What is the difference between someone who allows their sorrows and problems to drown them and someone who seems to rise above all their challenges? Oftentimes, the difference is a grateful heart.

A grateful heart will make your giants look like ants on the ground. With a grateful heart, you are unstoppable. Who can stand in the way of someone with a positive perspective that can't be shaken? No one!

But what do you do when you feel hopeless? What if you're speechless in time for prayer?

Start counting. Begin counting your blessings BY NUMBER. Shift your focus away from failure and began adding up all of your wins. Every day, at least twice a day, sit down and list your blessings, counting them by number. Just like when we count our complaints, let's flip the script and instead count our blessings.

Can't find anything to be grateful for? Take a look around you and break out in a praise:

- *I'm grateful that the sun is shining*
- *I'm grateful for shelter*
- *I'm grateful for life*
- *I'm grateful for breakfast on my table this morning*
- *I sent my family on their way and they made it safely, thank you!*
- *I'm grateful for my good health*

Joy is a medicine and when you begin to give thanks, even in the (seemingly) little things, the heaviness seems to magically lift and your mood becomes lighter.

Gratitude is your superpower. When you take a few moments to channel that power every day, you will become a much happier person, fully armed to take on whatever challenges come your way.

A great mentor of mine came into my life during a time of oppression. All I could see happening in my life was one disappointment after the next. I was expecting the worst. She suggested that I start a gratefulness journal and recommended I treat my oppression with grateful thoughts. Anytime you're being weighed down by troubles and feel depression seeping in, take this gratefulness antidote:

Gratefulness Antidote:

- Choose a notebook and make it your gratefulness journal.
- Each day when you awake, write down 3–5 things that you're grateful for each morning.
  (Side effects: At first this may be a bit challenging, especially during trying times.)
- Before you go to bed at night, return to that journal and write down 5 more things you're grateful for.
  (Side effects: By the next morning, you'll find that you have another 5 things to be grateful for.)
- Each day, as you continue to express your gratitude in writing, twice per day, begin to set your intention on finding things to be thankful for.
  (Side effects: Your subconscious mind will begin blocking out negative thoughts and instead hunt for the positives in each day.)

What's great about this journal is that it's your written record of the positive things that are happening for you and to you each day. If you get off track (and we all do from time to time), you can revisit your journal of positive thoughts and be reminded of all the good things in life.

One day at a time. One thought at a time.

Thinking negative thoughts on a regular basis creates a not-so-good thinking pattern. You'll have to develop new patterns in order to break old thinking habits and begin cultivating more positive thoughts. It may not happen overnight, but it can certainly happen. Before I began counting my blessings and keeping a gratefulness journal, it felt more natural for me to expect the worst vs expecting the best for my life. Some will try to make this change overnight and get discouraged when the change isn't permanent.

Just like it took work to develop negative thinking patterns, it will take some time to undo these habits and think more positively.

Instead of taking your negative thoughts one day at a time, take them on one thought at time.

We must constantly be replacing negative thinking with positive thinking around the clock. Treat it as a game and have some fun. The more you practice, the easier it will become to choose better thoughts. Take each thought one at a time, and choose your thoughts wisely. Watch your life transform.

To get the mind Power you need to overcome in hard times, remember to be great:

- Giants come, but are no greater than you are destined to be. Know that your giants are only as great as the giant you will become — and your battles are only as great as your greatness.
- Realize & Remember that all challenges come to an end eventually. Take a look into your past at all the things you went through and survived. Remember you're an overcomer.
- Elevate your mind by reaching inside and finding gratitude in the midst of what you're going through. Yes, it feels crazy while in the process, but keep saying, *"I'm grateful that I went through that; I'm getting ready for my blessing. I'm going to get on the other side. I'm grateful for how strong this is going to make me. I'm grateful for all the lives that will change and improve as a result of my going through this."*
- Allow yourself to learn all you need to during this trial in your life. There is a deeper meaning and greater purpose in all you're going through. Reach out and grab it. Embrace the change.
- This too shall pass. Focus your mind on the desired end. Believe that you can get through and that you will overcome.

"Win on the battlefield of your mind, and you've won!"

Chapter 9:
Pay it Forward

Ever wondered why some people always seem to have the sun shining on them? The ones we secretly envy. They've got the perfect life, perfect spouse and the perfect picket fence around the perfect house. Their businesses seem to achieve massive success overnight and life is being served to them on a silver platter. When they enter a room the atmosphere seems to transform instantly and people are sticking to them like flies on honey.

You can't always believe what meets the eye. What you see isn't always what you get.

Some of those "perfect people with the perfect life" have truly paid the price to get where they are today. We have no idea what they had to go through to get through. Many of those who are walking in the fruitfulness of the blessing are reaping a harvest from the many seeds they've sown.

This brings me to the first law of blessings. It's not possible to receive with a tightly closed fist! Want the floodgates to open in your life? Dare to enter each day seeking someone to bless. Those who operate in the blessing are not only open to receive, but are also ready to willingly give.

Sidebar: While there are huge full-time givers who go into their day seeking whom they can bless, there are also those who spend most of their time taking from others. People like this take and then take some more, while leaving you feeling used, exhausted and drained. Be very careful of non-reciprocal relationships while on your quest to be a blessing to others.

I took on a challenge along with a dear friend of mine. The challenge involved giving something to at least one person each day. Even if we only had one single dollar to give, we would pay it forward. This could be a total stranger in passing on the street or someone close to us. The challenge was designed to help us focus on being more intentional about our blessings. Sometimes when we aren't intentional, we just might overlook paying forward that small act of kindness.

To follow through with this challenge, I decided to set my intention on blessing someone on a particular Friday. That day was payday for my assistant. I decided to be intentional and pay her forward a bonus on top of her pay just to say thank you. Then, the following day, I blessed my mom. I went on throughout that weekend paying it forward to a few strangers as I went about.

The following Monday, after getting in the groove of intentionally blessing others, I picked up the mail and at that moment, right there at the mailbox, I'm met with adversity. You see, sometimes after we are obedient and sow seeds into the lives of others, we're faced with opposition. The letter I received was from my lawyer and inside was an unexpected bill of a couple thousand dollars. It seemed as though we'd just finished paying him the same amount, if not more, and there I was, after intentionally blessing one person after another, faced with disappointment.

Have you ever noticed that just after doing a good deed, instead of reaping good, you seem to reap bad? It's in these misleading moments that your faith is being tested. You have the choice to react in response to what it "seems" like or to stand still and know that the blessing is already yours.

It's important during these moments that you not be moved or discouraged. I know this can be easier said than done. Wouldn't it be great if everything were perfect? I'm here to encourage you, and it isn't over until it's over.

To continue on with my story, I went about ranting and complaining; throwing a tantrum like one of my children. I went to my mom to vent and she quickly stopped me in my tracks, reminding me not to be moved. I was uptight. My husband and I were preparing to leave for Mexico and the bill had me outraged.

Once I cooled down a bit, I decided to calmly give my lawyer a call to ask him about the unexpected debt. This was one of the quickest phone calls I've had in my life. My lawyer let me know that the bill was a complete mistake, wished me a good day and we ended the conversation.

I stood there motionless, still holding the phone in my hand as if the conversation hadn't ended. I was speechless, in awe of what had just happened. Let me tell you, I jumped the gun and got ahead of my blessing and got into fear. I immediately shifted into disbelief and frustration once it seemed I wasn't reaping the benefits of my intentional blessings.

That's a prime example of just what fear does to you. **My dad would always remind me of this acronym when we talked about fear:**

False

Evidence

Appearing

Real

He taught me this acronym when I was a girl and even to this day it holds true. Fear is belief in what it simply looks like; seems like. It isn't based on any real solid evidence and oftentimes, the very thing you fear hasn't happened yet and many times it won't ever happen. Remember, if it hasn't occurred it doesn't exist.

Back to my intentional blessings story. Let me just say, the blessings didn't stop there. The very next day, following the lawyer bill scare, I went to one of my favorite coffee spots. I went to pick up my favorite: iced vanilla latte and banana nut bread. The ultimate snack. I entered the drive-through line and placed my order, but when I pulled up to pay, the girls at the window looked super confused. They looked at one another, whispered a bit and then gave me the news, *"The manager said your coffee is paid for. Have a great day!"* I didn't know the manager, but I said, *"Thank you"*, pulled off and enjoyed that free bread and latte!

Some would label that as a small blessing, but not in my book. I believe in counting my blessings by number. *Free* looks like *favor* to me.

The favor continued throughout the day as I whisked in and out of stores. Strangers were showering me with kindness. One of my favorite affirmations is:

"I give and receive love everywhere that I go"

And that's just what I did. Be intentional about counting your blessings, every single one of them, and when adversity comes, be on standby and don't waver in your faith. Also, get EXCITED about blessing others. I even get my children excited about giving by allowing them to give tips when we eat out and money to those in need. They are cheerful givers and they look forward to witnessing a smile on someone's face when they give.

God says, He loves a cheerful giver. When you bring joy to others, magically you receive a double dose of joy right back. My husband never refuses the hand of a beggar, and if he has change he never holds it back. In the past, I couldn't understand it, but now I do the same. Give thanks, in even the (seemingly) little things, pay it forward and count your blessings by number.

If you find a dime on the street, say, *"Thank you!"*

If someone pays you a compliment, say, *"Thank you"* and count it as a blessing!

Your gratitude determines your latitude.

Be primarily concerned (consumed) with giving and not receiving. Stop calling certain blessings small and others big. Choose to perceive a blessing, no matter the size, a blessing. God will always give us what we need when we need it if we trust Him. He's always right on time.

Philanthropists give and do so freely. Some celebrities dress as if they don't have a dime, but they are intentionally giving to charities. A big reason they are so blessed is because they've adapted the spiritual laws of blessing.

Another thing to consider, we don't always receive in the same manner in which we give. Let's just say you want to grow oranges. Do you plant an orange to get an orange? No. You plant seeds! For instance, you may give of your time and, in turn, reap a return of money. You may give someone a monetary gift and in turn receive the blessing of a new home. The return may not be received in the same manner in which you gave, but it's just what you need and it's always right on time.

Blessings should always flow out to others. Others should also benefit from the blessings you receive. Blessings were never designed to benefit you only. They were designed to cover not just you, but even those connected to you will be blessed.

When we bless others, in turn, we are blessed. You reap what you sow. What you give you shall receive. Karma. Universal Law. There are many names for this principal. When you intentionally bless others, a blessing is on its way to you. It's a spiritual law. The more we are blessed, the more responsibility we have to bless others.

You've been blessed to be a blessing, so always remember to pay it forward.

“*To get the full value of joy, you must have someone to divide it with.*” — Mark Twain

Chapter 10:
Choose Joy

“*You have 24 hours in a day to make it the greatest day you ever lived.*” — Pastor Dustin Harper (my big brother)

You've been assigned this mountain to show others it can be overcome. The pain you have been feeling can't compare to the joy that's coming!

Your life lessons are often not just for you.

Sometimes we try to solve our problems by looking externally, but often the real problems are happening internally. There's one single choice that can change your life and propel you into your highest success:

Choose joy!

A lot of us go through our lives searching for what makes us truly happy. We are looking for happiness and seeking peace in relationships, food, money and many others things of this physical world. Many of us have thought:

If I could just get enough money, I'll be happy.
If I could just find Mr. Right or Mrs. Right, then I'll be happy.
Once I buy a new home, I'll be happy.
Once I land a new job, I'll be happy.
Once my business takes off, I'll be happy.

You know what happens? Once you get that new job, or business sales start to rocket, or you find the love of your life, there will still be times you're not happy and you will move the benchmark to something else.

Choose joy!

Make joy your number one choice. Aspire to have joy above material things. Material things fade away, but joy is overflowing. Joy is a state of mind and it is indeed a choice. Truly happy people have found something much deeper than a temporary feeling, and that's a joy that flows within. It doesn't matter if money is low or high, they still have joy. It doesn't matter if the sky is gray or blue, they still find joy. Material things and current circumstances don't change the state of their happiness.

Joy is a choice you can make each and every day! Joy is intentional. Joy comes from the inside and is everlasting. If you choose to tap into what you already have inside and nurture that joyful state of being, you'll begin living in a lasting positive emotional state that reaches beyond temporary feelings of happiness.

We make decisions every day; everything we say and do is a result of our decisions. For every choice, big or small, there's no easy formula for making the right decision. However, our lives begin to change the moment we decide to follow our heart's desires and what truly makes us happy. Happiness is a choice. Choosing *happy* means that we don't have to wait for everything to be perfect, nor control anything outside ourselves to maintain this positive state of mind. Something beautiful happens when we intentionally create a positive mindset and constantly choose joy.

Even when you don't feel it, begin to command attention to your emotions and begin to speak it:

"I'm wonderful. I'm excellent.
Today will be a phenomenal day!"
"Today is full of limitless possibilities."
"I'm open to receiving miracles today."

Joy is a choice that can be made every second of every day.

Begin living a happy life with these eight intentional actions:

1. **Count your blessings.** Blessings usually come in different forms, shapes and sizes. Seize the moment and count each blessing that happens in your life. I even count compliments, as they are blessings too.
2. **Smile.** It costs you nothing to smile and smiling sends positive vibrations and healing energy throughout your body. Smile at yourself too! Don't be afraid to smile each time you pass a mirror. Smiling is a great way to silently spread love everywhere and to even love yourself.
3. **Speak into your own life daily.** Shower yourself with loving compliments and practice positive affirmations. Instead of waiting for someone else to affirm us, let's take our power and begin affirming ourselves. Affirm all the positive things that you are each time you pass a mirror. Affirm all the positive characteristics you have, even when you don't feel you're displaying them yet. Start by telling yourself how great you are. Look

yourself in your eyes and say that you're more than capable, more than enough and more than able to make that thing happen.

4. **Command your morning.** Wake up on your own terms. Take a few extra minutes at the brink of each day giving yourself exactly what you need to have the best day ever. Prioritize those things you enjoy doing. Even though I have three kids who need my time and attention quite a bit, I'm very protective of my mornings and wake up on my own terms. Waking up early to make time for my morning routine allows me to fine tune my mind and go into my day with power.
5. **Exchange complaints for praise!** When we constantly complain, we only attract more situations into our lives to complain about! Have an attitude of gratitude and appreciate all that you have. When you catch your mouth forming to make a complaint, turn it immediately into praise and thanksgiving. A positive attitude will increase your performance and attract positive results.
6. **Complete at least one productive task per day.** We feel great when we've finished. Sometimes, we're so busy multitasking that once we are facing the completion of the day, we realize we haven't completed anything at all. Completion is a great feeling and contributes to our happiness. Before you go to sleep at night, think over the productive tasks that you've finished and give thanks, even if it's only that one productive task. One is much better than none. Just think: at the end of 30 days you'll have finished 30 productive tasks.

7. **Love thy neighbor as thyself.** Make an effort to respect even the unrespectable. Treat others the way you wish to be treated. I'm sure you've heard this said once or twice. It's probably one of the oldest in the book, but it's a great way to live and love. If you do good to others, good will return to you tenfold. Doing good to others produces more happiness and joy not only in you, but the world around you.
8. **Find purpose in your pain.** Use your pain as a footstool to accomplish a greater PURPOSE. I had to work through, walk through and learn to DANCE through my pain. A single perspective change can give you the power you need to get through painful times and walk fully in your purpose.

"This pain isn't breaking me, it's making me."

Remind yourself: *"I might be uncomfortable right now, but I'm going to stay positive because this is coming to an end. I'm going to get through this with flying colors and I'm going to soar right over it. This situation isn't breaking me. It's making me into a better, stronger, more compassionate version of myself."*

Chapter 11:
You've Got the Power

I have experienced several major setbacks in my life. A failed marriage, and that cut deep. I never expected to be a single mother; that one cut even deeper. These experiences had me questioning my beliefs. I felt like a failure.

Then, later down the road and all too son, I lost my dad.

I've heard it said that if it doesn't kill you it makes you stronger, and I am convinced that LIFE is the best teacher. The more we go through, the more life lessons we learn, and the more we learn and overcome, the greater our testimony. Yes, life doesn't always play fair and can knock you off your feet. But the first lesson learned when riding a bike for the first time is how to fall and get back up. Once you've fallen down, scraped your knee, gotten back up and learned to ride a bit longer, then you're ready to go the distance.

When you're in pain, how do you push through to your purpose?

The first test is when you're faced with the choice to either show up or not show up at all. There are times I don't feel strong, but even then I show up strong. I've learned to push even in those moments when I'm breaking inside. I reach deep down inside, take the negative energy and turn it into a positive feeling.

> "*Adopting the right attitude can convert a negative stress into a positive one.*" — Hans Selye

What keeps me going, is knowing that someone else out there is going through something way worse than I am currently. The pain I'm experiencing is happening to me and for me, and it's not more than I can bear. I show up into my day, because I know there's someone out there who needs me to be strong so that they can also show up strong. If I don't push through, someone else may die as a result of my quitting.

There were many days that, regardless of how torn apart I felt, I still had to show up for my students and followers. I still had to speak, encourage and teach. I still had to push through.

What if you don't have any cheerleaders, but you're always cheering for somebody else? What if you're literally crying, dragging yourself out of bed and not wanting to see the light of day? What do you do when life jabs you to the left and then to the right? It may seem hard. It may even seem impossible, but you show up and continue to press your way through.

I know it's easier said than done. It's hard to acknowledge your power when you're feeling powerless. It's hard to stand up and be strong for someone else when you feel all hope is gone. But I'm here to tell you that just because you feel faithless it doesn't mean you're devoid of faith.

Getting through what you're going through calls for tough skin. You'll need emotional strength.

Here are 7 steps to emotional toughness:

1. **Don't waste time feeling sorry for yourself.** Could we spend an entire day crying over spilled milk? We sure can. But my question for you today is: Does it really help? We could spend our every moment sobbing our

eyes out and questioning God, but tell me, what would it change? There are doors in our lives that are meant to be closed. Every chapter has an ending. There's a blessing underway. Trust the process.

2. **Don't resist change.** Sometimes growth hurts, and change pretty much ALWAYS hurts. What's more, a whole truckload of problems showed up after I helped others shift. Many times it seems our blessings are being blocked, but in all actuality, it's us who are doing the blocking. We pray for change, but we aren't doing any changing. The emotionally strong GROW, even when the growing gets tough.
3. **Don't waste energy on things you can't control!** That man; that woman; that friendship; that outcome cannot be controlled by you, let it go. People don't belong to us. Outcomes don't even belong to us. It's time to release those problems and people that we weren't responsible for creating in the first place. Remember, the only person you can control is yourself and your own response to the situations that happen.
4. **Don't be a people pleaser.** No matter what you do, some people still aren't going to be happy. My momma always told me to be sure I'm pleasing God and loving myself when making life decisions. At the end of the day, that's all that matters. I've taken that advice to heart and now I'm paying it forward to you. Be a God pleaser, and you can't go wrong.
5. **Don't make the same mistakes over and over.** And over (had to reiterate)! Learn from your mistakes. Get better and do better next time. Another momma-ism: as an adult, you can only make a mistake once, the second

time around, it's a bad choice. If you make a bad choice, don't waste time rolling around in the dirt for long. Dust yourself off and do better next time.

6. **Don't resent the success of others.** Don't compare your day 1 to someone else's day 100. Don't give away your power comparing yourself to others. Give praise to those who succeed and stay busy expecting blessings. When you focus on the positives, those blessings will hit your doorstep in good time. God's timing is perfect timing and your blessings belong to you.
7. **Don't expect immediate results.** I'm sure you've heard it said that "good things take time." The birth of a child takes nine long months but when they arrive words can't describe the beauty beheld. You'll go through pregnancy seasons when you carry that seed of greatness. Birthing requires nurturing, patience and perseverance. You'll have to bear with your blessings and allow them time and space to turn, kick, scream, and cry. That's just what babies do in the womb. It will take time and it won't feel good, but in due time that blessing is going to come to fruition. Allow yourself to be uncomfortable for a time and ride out the rough times. Not only are you going to be blessed in due time, but your entire circle will be blessed along with you.

The key here is to turn your negatives into positives and realize that just because you feel powerless, you've still got the power. You hold the keys within to your own success. You're in the driver's seat. You are in full control. Even when it doesn't feel great. Push through, show up and the blessings will flow.

Chapter 12: The 3 P's (Pain, Purpose, Power)

Through pain, I found my purpose.

Just as pain in the body is symptomatic of a deeper problem, it's the same for emotional pain. Symptoms such as bad relationships or lack of self-love reveal the existence of underlying issues. Looking back over some of my bad choices as a young adult, I've realized I didn't love myself. I believe some of the pain I experienced was a catalyst for self-discovery and self-love. If I hadn't learned to love myself early on, I wouldn't be where I am today and possibly could have driven myself over the deep end.

I've been asked if I regret any of my struggles. Do I regret having a child or being a single mom for a time? My answer is always, *"No"*. From the experience of being a young mom and with the changes that followed, what I've gained is priceless. I've gained self-esteem. I've gained self-love. I've gained confidence and began walking in my power. While losing so much, I've gained so much more; all the things I'd lacked before.

When times got tough, I could have easily thrown in the towel. I could have easily given up on everything, but I've learned, I've grown and I've evolved. If you would have put the old me into some of my current struggles, I wouldn't stand a chance.

Your struggles aren't meant to break you; they're meant to challenge and change you.

The journey of loving ourselves and growing through what we grow through doesn't stop once we've discovered more about ourselves. Trouble didn't stop coming once I learned to love myself. As a matter of fact, troubles have never stopped trying me. Are there still times I feel faithless? Yes! However, I've learned to reach deep down within myself and maybe even a bit beyond myself to find just enough faith to begin believing again. I want the same for you. In moments of despair, I pray that after reading these words you begin to stop in the midst of your pain and begin asking why? Do some soul-searching; dig deep within. Seek answers while in the low valley. Ask yourself, *"What can I learn from this?"*

Refuse to allow what you're going through to break you. Don't allow the pain of the past to get in your way and become a roadblock to your success. Refuse to allow your pain to shut you down and shut your mouth. I don't know if you know yet, but you've got a story to tell. Refuse to allow your pain to forbid you from encouraging others. There are people depending on your survival story so that they can find the strength to survive. Refuse to be stopped. Become allergic to quitting. Allow your pain to drive you to go even harder. Allow it to motivate you to push even further. Allow your pain to help you work through your flaws and build the best character in you.

I don't understand everything about life and I don't have all the answers. None of us do. One thing I do know, as a result of persevering, even in the things I didn't understand, I'm a stronger person today. Through my low valleys, I've shifted. Something has changed in me and it's so profound that others can see it. People have said, *"Wow, I appreciate your strength, but I would have never thought you were going through that."* Those around me didn't know what I'd been going through because I didn't suffer out loud. Challenges come, but you have the choice to allow them to knock you off your feet or not. My dad always said, "When life gives you jab after jab, put your boxing gloves on, stand up and keep fighting. Don't hang up your gloves. Don't get out the ring." Keep yourself planted by maintaining that unbreakable positive perspective. That contagious unfaltering positive energy. Always examine how you can grow and ask yourself, *"How can I grow from this?"* Allow yourself to go through in order to get through. Allow the pain to simply become your fuel.

Grow through what you go through

In this book, you may have noticed I've repeated these words over and over again. But we get better through practice. We become masters at success through repetition. Remind yourself repeatedly that you're a champion and it isn't over until it's over.

I'm blessed to say, that once I decided to give adversity a run for the money, I've been growing at record pace. I look back on my past and think on the times when I really thought I was at my lowest point. I really thought those trials were the worst things that could have happened, but you know what? I got through. Know what else? I've gone through more challenging times and made it through those too. I'm right here. I'm still standing! And you know what else? You are too!

Whenever we're going through a rough time, that time always feels like the toughest of them all. When you're weathering the storm, it always feels like the worst disaster ever. But once you make it through to the other side, to the clear skies, you take a glimpse at yesterday and smile. Within the blinking of an eye you'll find yourself standing on the other side of the storm. You made it! You survived the storm! And now you can see the rainbow.

Even now, when I walk through a low valley, I choose FAITH, once again. I look back and realize, God has never left me, He never will, and I got through. I'm confident in knowing that this storm will blow over and, as a result, I'll be much stronger. I remind myself of just how blessed I am and count my blessings. This wasn't my reality some time ago. Pain has brought me to this place of strength — and yours can too.

Remember to always stop, seek and ask yourself:

"What do I need to learn from this?"
"How can I turn this situation into a positive in my own life?"

I think that once you do it for YOU, you can then begin to pay it forward. *"How can I help others through this?"* When you start asking these types of questions, you start getting answers. By helping others, you focus less on your own pain. When you start helping others, you help yourself. When you see other people improving and being impacted by your story, it in turn strengthens you.

I still have my sad days, but I'm a bit stronger. I'm walking more fully in my purpose. That painful period in my life pushed me right out of my comfort zone, but I embraced it. I opened myself up to possibilities. I put myself in position to change in the middle of the pain I was going through. I found purpose in it. I asked questions. I sought answers.

> “*If you don't fulfill your purpose, someone may die*” — Kymberly Smith

Right now, today, I'm asking you: *what is your true purpose and are you in alignment with that purpose? We may be many things to a lot of people, but in reality who are we to ourselves? Are you staying true to your purpose in ALL that you do in life?*

When you began to walk out of your old self and into purpose, those who once knew you may not recognize you anymore. You'll be boldly speaking your truth and living life without limits. All those connected to you will experience a surge and be inspired to change. Walking fully in your purpose may make some people uncomfortable and that's just fine. Know you're on the right track.

Begin talking with others about what you do, why you do it and watch sparks fly. When you speak about the things you're passionate about you should get excited! Give yourself a reason to look forward to getting out of bed each morning. Don't be ashamed to shout it to the rooftops and share your story. You never know who may be in need of a lifeline.

A painful past has propelled me into an excellent future. And suddenly, I was shaken out of my shell. I realized I may not have until tomorrow. I realized, I have a voice and that I need to be heard. We all have gifts, but if we're hoarding them and holding them inside, who are we really changing? What legacy are we leaving behind?

Ask yourself today, every day and in all that you do, *"Am I fulfilling my true purpose?"* Even if you're stuck in a job you hate and surrounded with circumstances you wish you could change, ask yourself, *"Am I living or am I just existing?"*

Before I embraced the pain and began seeking the lesson, I was merely floating; existing; not living fully. I spent more time reliving the past than I did enjoying the present. Now that I live for something, there's this spark in all that I do. All that I do is an extension of divine purpose.

Our lives aren't meant to be spent alone. We weren't put here on earth to only save ourselves. There's a sense of fulfillment that comes when we dedicate time to helping others. I've found my true purpose and will be forever evolving, growing and I want for others to have the same beautiful experience.

New awakenings are birthed within us over and over and each time we break through, something new is on the horizon.

We have more power in our pinky finger than the snares that come to befall us. What makes us so powerful is doing what we do, but with a purpose. Remember, you have a story to tell. You have a WHY; a reason to show up and do what you love doing. Being mindful of this WHY helps you show up and show up STRONG.

If you don't do *you* to the fullest and show up strong, who else will? We gain our strength when we learn to embrace the 3 P's: Pain, Purpose and Power. You're stronger than you know. You got this.

Chapter 13:
Tools

Sometimes we just have to go through until we get through. During those times, when we're weathering the storm it's good to have some tools to keep you afloat. Here's your survival kit packed with tools to take you from your painful times into power and purpose. Feel free to dig into the toolbox whenever you need.

Tool #1 – Do something NEW

During hard times, you may find yourself miserably doing the same thing day in and day out. Trying to pass time during a down season can feel like an eternity. It may be best to switch up your routine! Pick up a new book, a new hobby, support group or friend. Take up a Zumba class; travel to a new place. Be spontaneous and don't be afraid to try something new. Focusing on the new will refocus your mind towards the new season that's coming. Release the problem and focus on providing yourself a new experience you'll enjoy in this moment.

Tool #2 – Practice self-care and self-love, always

And this doesn't just go for the women. Men, this also applies to you! Do something good for you. It could be a walk in the park, a day at the beach, a nice healthy smoothie or spa day. It doesn't have to be an extravaganza. A warm cup of tea, in front of the fire place; curled up with your favorite book will suffice. Whatever makes you happy. It's all about giving yourself what you enjoy most while maintaining your ultimate health. Make a date with yourself. Put it on the calendar, and don't you dare cancel.

Tool #3 – Press pause!

In those confusing moments when I'm on the wall and find myself fighting with myself, I'm moving in circles with nervous energy, not sure what to do. When I'm unsure of my next move, that's when it's necessary to call a time out! Taking a pause doesn't always require large amounts of money spent or an exquisite getaway. It's simply doing less of what's stressing you and more of what nurtures you. When you've called a time out, it's time to give yourself more of what fuels your joy and take that much needed time to rest, reflect, focus and cultivate new ideas.

Tool #4 – Affirmations are your friend

This deserves an entire section within itself, so I will elaborate a bit more on this one. Affirmations are very powerful and have changed my life from barely making it to making life great. I accredit much of my evolution and transformation from the inside out to my commitment to saying, reading and meditating on positive thoughts and words.

You see, when you affirm things (**call** the **things** that are **not as though they are**); when you affirm the GOOD within and about yourself, it changes your perspective and shifts your focus from negative to positive. I believe that positivity exists in everyone. Moreover, I believe we've all been created in the positive image of the Creator, and that positive light exists on the inside of us. It's always there, even during tough times. Sometimes you'll have to reach a bit deeper to pull on that power; tap into your spiritual eyes to see.

Affirmations are when you make positive statements about yourself and your life in the present moment. So, for instance, if you are insecure, your statement could be: *"I am completely confident and secure."* It's an *"I am"* statement. "I am" is an 'in the now moment' statement. It speaks in the present tense, as though it's happening right now, not in some future that hasn't arrived yet. It's the real truth about yourself and what you *desire* for yourself to be. Affirmations are when you talk about what you see within yourself through your spiritual eyes.

I had just about given up on myself when God sent me a human angel. This was an elderly lady who spoke words of life when I thought life wasn't possible. She wrote me a prescription for worry and stress. I'd like to pay that antidote forward.

This human angel wrote my very first affirmation. In fact, she wrote ten of them. They were all about overcoming the nervousness I felt, releasing bad relationships, loving myself and carrying myself in such a way *"as if I owned the earth."* She had me affirm about taking back my power. She wrote affirmations about money because, at that time, I was struggling financially.

She gave me this exact affirmation formula and I'm passing it along to you:

AFFIRMATION FORMULA

Write out these 10 affirmations, 10 times before bed each night. Say them aloud in the morning, 10 times each. Think about these affirmations during each day.

Then she challenged me: *"Do this daily for thirty days and watch your life change."*

Before I knew it, my life completely transformed and I am still amazed by the power that affirmations have had over my life.

Here are a few of my favorite prescriptions (affirmations) to take during hard times.

Practice retraining your mind and your mouth by saying, meditating and writing these down several times a day:

"I give and receive love everywhere that I go. Everyone loves me. I am safe."

"I deserve the very best."

"Love comes to me in the perfect time and space."

"I am living my very best life right now."

"I carry myself as one who owns the earth, because I do."

Don't let the list stop here. Affirmations are indeed very powerful and they can be customized and made personal to manifest your highest good.

Tool #5 – Give Thanks

Live in gratitude and give thanks, even in the (seemingly) little things. **Remember the gratefulness antidote:** After you're done writing your affirmations each night, sit, reflect and write five things from that day that you're grateful for. You may feel silly doing this at first. You may even struggle to find more things to be grateful for. This was me in the beginning. Over time, you'll begin noticing a shift in your energy. You'll begin changing your energy from negative to positive because subconsciously, you're retraining your mind and spirit to believe the best of yourself and your situation.

Tool #6 – Choose Health

Ask yourself, *"How can I live a healthier life?"* I don't think many of us realize that the way we eat and treat our bodies have such a great effect on how our mind functions and how good we feel. As I began changing my mindset, I also began changing my lifestyle by making healthier choices for myself and family. I gave up sugar and a lot of other unhealthy habits. When you eat well, exercise and get into nature, you begin to feel just like a million bucks. What you put in eventually comes out. This not only goes for your words, thoughts and what you accept as truth, but also relates to the foods you eat. Personally, my health epiphany happened once I lost my dad. I allowed losing him to be my motivation for healthy eating and living. I've gotten more serious about me. When you eat well you look good and when you look good you feel good. Make healthy choices that bring out the best in you.

Tool #7 – Help Others

Once you've helped and supported yourself, then you can begin directing your positive energy towards others. Maybe some of the negative energy you're feeling can be shifted into positive by helping others.

Remember, it isn't linear. At first, it's okay to feel stuck and even angry. I always encourage people to allow themselves the right to "feel what they feel". Give yourself the time and space to mourn or grieve. Most people are not going to lose a relative today and become "Captain America" tomorrow. It's quite normal to not feel so great and also feel stuck during hard times. The key is, once you've allowed yourself time to grieve a loss, whatever your specific loss may be, it's time to accept that all things must come to an end. This includes your sorrow. Turn your pain into positives by focusing on helping someone outside of yourself and by paying it forward. Reaching beyond yourself and into the life of others lightens your load and lifts your mood.

Tool #8 – Watch Your Circle

I attended a women's conference last summer with a friend and some powerful words stuck out for me. Attending reaffirmed what I've learned over time about circles. Make sure that your circle is strong and full of positive like-minded people who are either where you want to be, or getting there with you. First, believe in yourself. Believe that you're already a powerhouse, you're effective and that you're climbing heights. Instead of keeping company with those who constantly drain you, cling to those who add value to your life instead. Oh, and always remember to remain valuable.

When the unforeseen happens, many of us get stuck for extended periods of time because we refuse to seek the a deeper meaning and learn the lesson. We wallow in our sorrows and allow them to eat away at us from the inside out. When we begin seeking answers, opening up and learning to accept and process our feelings, something very beautiful can be birthed during our season of pain.

Once you turn inward, reflect and ask yourself how you can learn, improve and change, you become this transformational beacon of light that shines out into all the world around you.

Reaching within this toolkit and embracing your power during painful times will allow you to operate in much more confidence. These are your secret weapons when on the battlefield. You'll stop feeling sorry for yourself and begin finding purpose through what you're going through. It's time to unleash the power within and step into the light.

Chapter 14:
Treasure

What are you sitting on?

I recently sat in bed one night and as I was reading the book *The Power of Now: A Guide to Spiritual Enlightenment* by Eckhart Tolle, I was inspired by this story:

> *Every day a man walked by a beggar who was sitting on top of a chest. He asked the guy: "Have you looked inside of that chest that you're sitting on?" The beggar said, "No, I just sit on it." He walked past him each day and asked him the same question. Finally, the beggar got up, opened the chest and found out the chest was full of gold!*

Will you believe that all of those years this beggar was crying out, begging for those who passed by to drop him pennies? He didn't realize all that he had inside of the chest that rested beneath him. All of those years he waited, hoping that someone in passing would change his situation when all along, he had a treasure within that could last him a lifetime.

Oftentimes, we tend to look outside ourselves for happiness. We believe there's that something or someone out there who will magically fix our unhappiness or feelings of unworthiness. When in reality, the only person who can rescue us from our limiting thoughts and beliefs about ourselves is us.

Right now, are you utilizing what you have on the inside? The treasure you have within can't be priced. It's priceless. A value can't be placed on it. The value goes on to infinity and beyond.

I want to leave you with these words: Whatever you've been seeking, praying for, longing for, I guarantee you that if you turn deep within and go inward, you'll find you've been sitting on a goldmine all along. Just dare to look.

The treasure lies within.

About the Author

Dallas Gordon, B.A. Theology, is an author, inspirational speaker and expert business coach. She's a proud wife and mom of three beautiful children.

Dallas dedicates her time to her passion for motivating others and inspiring them to reach their highest potential. Dallas also helps business owners increase brand awareness in the digital marketplace and increase traffic and sales. She encourages all those around her to live their fullest life and to embrace and monetize their passions. She's built successful companies and communities that encourage transformation and growth.

www.ingramcontent.com/pod-product-compliance
Ingram Content Group UK Ltd.
Pitfield, Milton Keynes, MK11 3LW, UK
UKHW021051270726
13967UKWH00012B/207

9 781912 551323